Prying Refried

Ppigpenn Press
2018 ©

CONTENTS

The City

Catfish McDaris

The Ass That Wouldn't Quit

If the Moon Had a Pussy I'd Fuck It Doggie Style

Cape Valentine

She Loved Me Because Of Poetry

Antelope Dream

Charles Bukowski

5437 2/5 Carlton Way
Los Angeles, Calif. 90027
1974

Writer and poet of international acclaim and renown. These four previously unpublished pieces were given to Jack Micheline in 1974, while Bukowski was living at the address mentioned above They were friends.

Help Wanted

divine grace of
circumstance-
the knife is back
again,
my radio sings to me;
drunk, I phone women in distant
places-
I speak, not knowing what I am
saying; I listen, I hear a voice,
but when I put the phone down
it is only a phone
and the walls look at
me.

all these women, holy jesus,
all these women everywhere
some of them are pissing
some of them are plotting
some of them are cooking beans

holy jesus
send me the one who is pissing

I need somebody to pull the
knife out

age 20 to 60
no experience necessary
will
train.

d.n.f.

they shot the horse
he kicked 4 times
with the bullet in his
brain
his skin shone
his skin sweated

they pushed him into a green trailer
pulled by a yellow tractor
driven by a man in a gray
felt hat

I walked back inside
and looked up the legs of a young woman
sitting and
reading the Racing Form

she made me hot

the dead horse had been my last
bet

my handicapping was going sour

then she saw me looking

I turned around
walked away

walked to a white water fountain
bent and drank.

Extant

the victim is the dog of man
the victim is dog the man
the victim is the dog man
the hot dog
mustard drizzling down the fingers
Lou Gehrig rockabye baby Lou
Ernie o Ernie o
Graziano and Zale
Zale and Graziano
blood on the hotdog
war
ha ha
war haha
Lookie all the wars
lookie lookie lookie
here comes cookie
all over the sheets
sheet metal workers
the victim is the workers
the victim is Eugene V. Hemingway Debs
Thomas Carlyle Jr.
Greta Garbo grabbing balls
let me acquaint you with fax:
ants ain't done got no chance
the Phillies need roller skates
Marilyn Monroe was a lesbian
my mother loved olives
spiders are ugly people
the government's going to raise taxes again
because they think we aren't poor enough
why, piss, kid, I been wearing the same pair of pants for
4 years
snorkle, we need more snorkle and weenie bakes and
blue moons
BLUE MOON OH BLEWEEWW MOOOOON HOW
I ADOOORRE YOU!
Patricia Hearst won't you please come home?

bow wow bow wow wow
bow wow bow wow wow
Peepee's got the chicken-pox
the waller's in the icebox
pop's comin' home drunk again tonight
the victim likes it
the victim is a tricycle

the victim is a gonorrhea face
the victim is a stick of gum wrapped in green
the victim is the queen's asshole

now look boy stop beating those drums
now look boy stop beating those drums
now look boy stop beating your meat
it's too hot in August
thank you, my man

one of the greatest goddamn shows you've
ever seen-
the spider lady sucks off the vanilla ice cream
man-
all for a dime
ten cents
or your mother's ruby nipples

I'd like to acquaint you with the fax:
Picasso was a rummy with cocoanut lodged in his
rectum
Schopenhauer (1788-1860) flogged off his cat
and kicked Marilyn Monroe's door down
55 miles an hour against gravity is like
licking your grandmother's cunt in a
sandstorm
Hitler didn't paint roses
he invented them
and he's down at the corner news-stand now
pinching pink little girls on their elbows
and sundry parts

I care for you, darling, I love you,
the only reason I fucked L. is because you fucked
Z. and then I fucked R. and you fucked N.
and because you fucked N. I had to fuck
Y.   But I think of you constantly, I feel you
here in my belly like a baby, love, I'd call it,
no matter what happens I'd call it love, and so
you fucked C. and then before I could move again
you fucked W., so then I had to fuck D.   But
I want you to know that I love you, I think of you
constantly, I don't think I've ever loved anybody
like I love you

bow wow bow wow wow
bow wow bow wow wow.

to weep in her hair

sweating in the kitchen
trying to hit one out of here
54 years old
fear bounding up my arms
toenails much too long
growth on side of leg

the difference in the factories was
we all felt our pain
together

the other night I went to see the
great soprano
she was still beautiful
still sexy
still in personal mourning
but she missed note after note
drunk
she murdered art

sweating in the kitchen
I don't want to murder art

I should see the doctor and get that thing
cut off my leg
but I am a coward
I might scream and frighten a child
in the waiting room

I would like to fuck the great soprano
I'd like to weep in her hair
I'd like to watch her walk to the bathroom

Polly wants a cracker
Popeye writes his phone number on shithouse walls:
"I suck young boys"

and there's Lorca still down in the road
eating Spanish bullets in the dust
the great soprano has never read my poems
we both know how to murder art
drink and mourn
sweating in the kitchen
the formulas are gone
the best poet I ever knew is dead
the others write me letters

I tell them that I want to fuck
the great soprano
but they write back about other
things
useless things
dull things
vain things

I watch a fly on top of my radio

he knows what it is
but he can't talk to me

the great soprano is dead.

Jack Micheline

Longtime artist and street poet born in New York and lived in San Francisco. He has performed with and been praised by an entire generation of writers and artists. Since first publication of this special edition of First Class, Jack has passed away.
"Micheline is a flowing, jostling master. A jew drunk singer, very fine. He knows best the betrayals, the pavements, the whores with lemon rinds up their bungs, and the lice in the spotlights."
-Charles Bukowski.

The Song of Kid Willie

Willie was nineteen when he first read "On The Road"
The next night at the non coms mess he faked a crack up and got
discharged
The smell of the fresh air and open sky sucked in his nostril
He grew long hair and went on the road
Hitchhiking to Cody Wyoming he fell in love with a waitress named
Beatrice
He made love to her in a barn on the outskirts of town
On the road his thin body against the wind and the night and sky
Susie from Samon blew him in a church
Arlene from Great Falls fondled his hair in a salt mine
Joan from Odessa
Eleanor from Yakima
Maureen from Portland
Fat Josephine from Vale
Louise from Eugene
The Timbers from Bellingham and Mt. Vernon
Stole a car in Eureka
Sell out at Big Sur
Picked grapes in Fresno
cotton in Bakersfield
Wrote his first poem in San Berdoo and swam in Big Bear
Fucked an Old German landlady in a furnished room in San Jose
Willie was turned on to grass, poetry, fresh air and cunt
He was six foot two and his long light brown hair flowed in the wind
Willie was in love with life and the sky
He kept asking people where Jack Kerouac was
Walked from Shoshone to Las Vegas
Flagstaff
Gallup
Tucumcari
Was pulled in for vagrancy in Amarillo
Fifteen days in the county jail
Met Jimmy the Greek who taught him to hop freights
Mobile

Gulfport
Biloxi
New Orleans
Got drunk on Olive Street St Louis and climbed the arch
Rema from Natchez
Sharon from Memphis
Paducah
Terre Haute
Valparaiso
Chicago he walked the hot pavement, the city streets
nose infected eyes bloodshot got stuck there three months
 fucking an indian made
  wrote blues

Topeka-one poem
Tucimcari-3 poems
Albuquerque-5 poems
Denver-got drunk
Medicine Bow-fasted 4 days
Juliette from Casper
Billings lost a shoe
Big Sandy-prayed on a mountain
White Fish-met two indians
East Port-went swimming
Tacoma-got laid 7 poems
Kelso-met a preacher's daughter
Monterey-got a job in a restaurant
 fell in love with skinny Georgine
 Georgine her strawberry hair and green eyes
Many chicks and many nights he wrote his poem on thigh bone of
hearts
sky, tree, wind, rain, clear skies ahead
his song of the open road
his song of love
farms
barns
shacks
O'grass
rivers

red dusks
and yellow sunsets
white houses in the night sky
The freights and horns and whistles, motorcycles
and the laugh of schoolgirls
their legs glistening in the sunlight
the smile of teasers
the fast quick pieces
and the cold look of priests
cool mountain streams
and waters of spring
O'shade of mountains
and stench of jails
dark and windless lockups
from here to Santa Fe
hard dick faces
sadist cops
Willie on the highway
Willie on the road
Sing the Song Kid Willie
The song of the road you love
He's out there on the skyway
He's out there with the stars
The playgrounds of the night and wild laughter
Yahoo!

Jack Micheline
Charlie's Pad
26 June 1968

My Philosophy

I was born on the street of lost fools
on a sunny winter's day
howling naked to the sky
with a pair of bright eyes from a crutch and anchor
I wandered through the cities in a daze
amid the rubble, noises, madhouse, prison, jail
twisting, running, hiding from the pack
a sassy hothead racing through the stretch
and found no answer, only in myself
that man was greed and rotten to the core
and nations came and went and so did causes
battles to be fought, the inner hell of doubts
The key was in the sunlight
a pair of thighs
a look
a glance
I chose the rebel's path
the back-streets of the soul
a magic pen on paper
a writer's scrawl
a painter's eye submerged with submarines and color
a swirling dervish of dream sublime
to hold the flower up amid the wars
to kiss the plunger down within the depths of hell
to raise this dungheap each one molecule
the waves of twilight blazing in the night
a child walking in the dusk of cities
and so I hid away to some dark place
a prisoner on a mountain-peak
and wrote my solitary song

June 12, 1975
San Francisco, CA.

Walking in Kerouac's Shadow

The alabaster city gleams in the sunlight
I am on a bus to Santa Rosa
Away from the stinking hotel
They tell me I am famous, like the Jerome cookies
Streets, poems, nuthouses, jails, paintings, con-men and time
My twenty years of poems and paintings
stored away in house and cellars
relentless with anger and love
I ponder at life and the world around me
The bus speeds on the highway going sixty
I am fifty-two, live alone, considered some mad freak genius
In reality I am a fucked up poet
who will never come to terms with the world
No matter how beautiful the flowers grow
No matter how children smile
No matter how blue is the bluest sky
The harsh realities of life, that life is mostly a put up job
The genius rain avoids us
The lone solitary soul that does her beautiful dance for all to see
I seek the genuine leaf blowing in the wind
The real person tapping a song whose melody
flows through rivers and time
The image that dance with stars
The sun that melts anger and harassment
Years spent begging and hustling
Carrying paintings on buses
Carrying mattresses through streets
Evictions, lost loves, hangovers, rheumatism, hemorrhoids
For a muse that rarely pays off
I must be mad, bewitched like a lost gambler
Down to my last bet with no carfare or candy
I am not subtle or charming
I cannot lie for money or tell stories
I'm the grey fox some shmuck
The old pro chasing the mad dream
The crazy Jew himself
Who didn't know when to quit

Who can't say die unless I die
It is all a mad dream
The race track full of maniacs
Lost gamblers living on hope and dreams
Tomorrow is never better
The same buses full of beaten and tired faces
I only know when the cock rises and the crow howls
To eat, to drink, to take a leak
And chicken is good to eat when one is hungry
Money buys everybody, that is why the world is fucked up
That is why politicians have seventeen faces and speechwriters
And waitresses wear lipstick
Why mediocrity rules
Why poets hang out in groups for protection
Why musicians disappear faster than flies
And artists suck the rich quicker than summer watermelons
and Bourgeois children
Why the communists and capitalists
Use the same deck of tricks
To hide the miraculous
The magic of life
The wonder of children and salamanders and birds
Wonder is the thunder
Wonder is the Spring rain itself
Wonder is the young girl in love
Wonder is love
The concerto
The hummingbird
The clouds moving across the night sky
It is raining again
Light against darkness
Shadows chasing the sun
The sun chasing the shadows
Man against the night
Man and woman together with the night
The day awakens
Let's sing a song
For those who chase the night
For those that dance with light

One speck of light
No matter who is light
Light the unknown
The unknown, it is all we have
Anything is possible
Like new born colors flashing across the Universe
The road
The vagabond
The dreamers
The dancers
The unsung
Fuck the Gung Ho!
Byron Hunt is doing a collage at the Goodman Building
Ed Balchowsky is doing another painting
Raising his one arm to the sky
Rosalie Sorrells is singing a song in Kansas
Sam Shepard is smiling
Rare birds are coming out with new coats of color
Rainy Cass is alive and well in New Orleans
Valentine Chuzioff is sketching some blond in Jackson Square
Bodenheim hustling another poem for wine
Franz Kline singing a sad song at the Cedar
Kerouac talking to the moon again
James T. Farrell chasing a waitress at Yankee Stadium
Chalie Mingus bopping, chukking, eating a steak
Playing bass with angels
Wilber Ware
Gil Gaulkins
Bill Bosio
Charlie Stark
Sue McGraw
Linda
Charlotte
Banana Boat
Steamboat Jones
Jeremiah
Jerusalem
The light is coming out
I'll give the sun away

It belongs to everybody
It's not mine to give away
Those with the sun
Those seeking the sun
Those on the run in the Chicago night
Those in jail
Those in the towers
Those chasing a ghost in the wilderness
Those on the road
Those with dreams
Those who will never give up
Those who are learning to dance
Those perplexed
     agonized
     wacked
     wretched
     tattooed
     confused
We are all the sun
You are the sun
This world is one
Those with wonder, you are the sun
Shake the sun
We are one
The moon and the Sun are brothers!

Tonight I Push My Wagon Into the Night Sky

Walking now on the lower East Side
It is Friday early evening
I stop at KIWI*"2
Jimmy's Bar
Four Poor Whites
Three unemployed actors
Six Professional drunks
A Carpenter
A Bike rider
A Poet
I go west to the sky
It starts to rain
drops of water on my head
We are all human I think
Each one tries to communicate
It is difficult in this city
To go beyond hello and goodbye
In Shanghai
Or Moscow
Or London
Or Amsterdam
Or Madrid
It is also difficult

Mario Lafont is a painter and poet
Jimmy Knighton is a poker player
Seven rummies stand under an awning drinking their wine
The rain is still coming down this day in October
Out in the country the leaves are turning colors now
The constellations are moving in the zodiac
There is this city too many sad beaten faces
It is good to be an optimist

But how, my lord, in Babylon does one affirm this darkness
I shake the cobwebs from my brain
I shake the belly swollen with scotch
I shake the rain

Let's do a dance mother
Let's kiss the waitress
She is nineteen
her name is Camille
Tonight I push my wagon into the night sky
Like a young child
I affirm the worm
I bite the apple of dreams
and send you my friends
who have come in the rain to hear me
better tidings for the world
A young boy smiles at his mother
I wish him luck and love in all horizons

New York City
October, 1967

The City

The city rose out of a flower
cunning and sharp
clothed in rag or top hat
dagger at its heart
the streets disguised with perfume scent or dung
the dreary compromise of its face
hardened as a pimp or financier
the middle classes drag their ass
the rich bored with excitement
the poor their dream strung like a clothesline
The city rose out of a flower
cunning and sharp
like a drunken street or a nowhere bar
down by the rocks they drink wine or kerosene
we have a choice how we die
cunning and sharp
clothed in rag or top hat
there is a dagger at your heart

Barcelona, Spain

Catfish McDaris

Born (1953-)
From: Albuquerque, New Mexico and
Milwaukee, Wisconsin.

The Ass That Wouldn't Quit

Her ass was fire
Her ass was the sun, the moon, a Tyrannosaurus Rex
Her ass laughed and cried

It could make brave men cowards
It could start wars
It could make rich men beggars

It could make saints into sinners
It could turn water into whiskey
It could make the rain come down

When she walked through the Louvre
It turned the Mona Lisa into The Scream.

Her ass was of biblical proportions
Her ass started playing kazoo, but soon
Mastered all wind required instruments
Including the slide trombone
Her ass made lions and bears roar with hunger

It was the Queen of Sheba doing the Twist
Cleopatra in her prime walking like an Egyptian
Marilyn Monroe in a sheer white dress

All the beauty that Paul Gauguin captured in Tahiti
The marlin that Santiago lost to the sharks
Babe Ruth's grand slam over center field

Her ass was Elvis Presley's blue suede shoes
Jimi Hendrix's guitar from Woodstock
It was Steve McQueen's motorcycle
From The Great Escape

A winning Powerball lottery ticket
The Hope diamond
It was all the words from Pablo Neruda,
Li Po, Tu Fu, and Sun Tzu's The Art of War

A saber tooth tiger, a killer bee, a Spanish fly
A zillion tarantulas crawling up the
Leaning Tower of Pisa

Her ass was the Great Pyramid at Giza,
Chichen Itza, the Taj Mahal, Stonehenge
Her ass was the Dallas Cowboy Cheerleaders
Naked doing cheers on the Great Wall of China

As her fine ass retreated
I poured gas all over my body
And waited for lightning.

If the Moon Had a Pussy I'd Fuck It Doggie Style

Why do scumbags
always seem to
break into your
house while you're
reading Bukowski
and trying to shit?

I'd written a poem
about Uncle Willy
trying to sodomize
me and I killed him

With the back of the
toilet. His eyeballs
rolled back into his
skull and resembled
hard boiled eggs.

What a shitty way to
go, motherfucker, he
should've picked
another house, when

I hit him he squawked
like a parrot in the dark
jungle that hadn't
learned to speak human.

Cape Valentine

Love is a runaway train
An elephant stampede
The Grand Canyon at sunrise
Van Gogh's bedroom
Good days bad sad dogs cats babies death
Beautiful intelligent enchanting intriguing
A memory of a memory
Back to back against the wall and the wolf
and the tax man and the ripper and the vultures
Mona Lisa's whisper and laughter
A hurricane of dreams on the precipice of life.

She Loved Me Because Of Poetry

I am wood, you are fire

I am the beach, you are the ocean
when you're in my arms, nothing is wrong

I'm lying on magic clouds, waiting for you
my love is clinging to the cliff by its fingernails

"My dog ate seven cockroaches,
do you think it will get sick?"

"Naw, I used to eat them squirming
bastards swimming in hot sauce
on tortillas down in Mexico, my cholo
would do the mezcalito sombrero dance"

Six mailboxes, a coyote and a ninja
with three eyes, Hercules, Copernicus
the fear of God and love of Lucifer
dynamite stew and a brass knuckle sandwich

A saber tooth tiger and nine ants
wearing red sneakers and an
electrified rooster monkey

Some search broken dreams and
empty bottles in vain for a past
path of bloody shadows and souls

Lonely phones ring, scream and beg
while sad blue poets have visions of terror
and insatiable ravenous tigers pacing the cage

Francisco Goya's Saturn Devouring His Son
and the Man Eating Mares of Diomedes, she made
her imitation Mona Lisa smile, threw back her

long dark hair and vanished into smoke.

Antelope Dream

Roberto had many stories, he told me he'd met
Antelope at a powwow in Gallup, she was unreal.
Camping in the Painted Desert, they traveled along

The Gila hitting Geronimo's raiding grounds. Antelope
was Chiricahua Apache. Roberto was related to Wilma
Mankiller of the Cherokee. Building a wickiup at a

Sulfur springs surrounded by peyote, they shapeshifted,
seeking visions. On top a carved mountain, they became
enveloped in a turquoise cloud. The mountain crumbled.

Buffalo and spotted horses stampeded, their hooves sounding
like thunder. In the sand were images of Washington, Jefferson,
Roosevelt, and Lincoln. Antelope and Roberto made love.

Printed in Poland
by Amazon Fulfillment
Poland Sp. z o.o., Wrocław